EXCERPTS FROM A

T0177124

# EXCERPTS FROM A BURNED LETTER

## JOELLE BARRON

**NIGHTWOOD EDITIONS**

2024

Nightwood Editions
P.O. Box 1779
Gibsons, BC VON 1VO
Canada
www.nightwoodeditions.com

COVER DESIGN: Evelyn Elgie
TYPOGRAPHY: Carleton Wilson
COVER PHOTO: *Le Sommeil*, Gustave Courbet, 1866

Nightwood Editions acknowledges the support of the Canada Council for the Arts, the Government of Canada, and the Province of British Columbia through the BC Arts Council.

This book has been printed on 100% post-consumer recycled paper.
Printed and bound in Canada.

LIBRARY AND ARCHIVES CANADA CATALOGUING IN PUBLICATION
Title: Excerpts from a burned letter / Joelle Baron.
Names: Barron, Joelle, 1990- author.
Description: Poems.
Identifiers: Canadiana (print) 20230582044 | Canadiana (ebook) 20230620698 | ISBN 9780889714700 (softcover) | ISBN 9780889714717 (EPUB)
Subjects: LCGFT: Queer poetry. | LCGFT: Poetry.
Classification: LCC PS8603.A7713 E93 2024 | DDC C811/.6—dc23

*for Katy*

# CONTENTS

*My love and I took hands and swore*
*Against the world to be*
*Poets and lovers evermore.*

—Katherine Bradley & Edith Cooper,
   writing as Michael Field, 1893

# SUNNY COVE

*I am more convinced than ever that we are shards of others.*
—Jenn Shapland

1

Like Benedetta of Vellano, I grew up remotely. Arrived
at Catholic sleepaway camp three months after the meningitis death
of my sister, my throat full of grief-thirst that received

no answering gulp. Benedetta's father promised her to God
in exchange for her mother's life, and at nine years old, she left
her mountain home to join a convent. Nightingales
that followed her were another word for bodies touching.

In northwestern Ontario, 2003, it was frog song
layered in the night-breath of girls.

Emotion drove into my hyoid bone, as if the butterfly
of my thyroid would rip apart its flesh cocoon, float bloodily

over the scream-bright water. At Sunny Cove, the slightly older teens
in charge woke us at dawn to bathe in Rainy Lake.
370 children shoved each other off the floating dock,

left rainbow trails of fruity shampoo. I didn't know
about Benedetta, or time, how it's not really moving forward.

The world looked movie-set fake, its fictional sun.
The lake was cold as a corpse, which I had recently learned
was surprising, but not unbearable.

3

Seventeenth-century nuns were bred for chastity and silence. A woman
was a vessel, in one way or another. Benedetta
married Christ, her wedding band a wound.

They made her abbess at thirty. Christ told her not to eat.
Bartolomea watched over Benedetta at night when Christ would come
and switch their hearts, though his was so large

it bulged divinely in the confines of her ribcage.

*4*

Camp theme that year was "It's My Life." Campers swayed nightly
in the hot chapel, canonizing Bon Jovi while mosquitos filled
our mouths and eyes with their tiny vibrations. Saint Tommy, Saint Gina,

deliver us from evil, maketh our hearts into open highways.
My sister's body hovered over me like a game of light as a feather,
stiff as a board. She was buried in her Lakehead tracksuit
and we wrote on her casket like a yearbook.

Slapped bugs against my arms, little explosions. How breakable
I was. Throat full of something I chose to believe
was the Holy Spirit.

Benedetta had many visions. When she lay down to sleep,
handsome young men would beat her body with swords and sticks
and chains. Christ told her the pain meant it was real,
like a B-movie anti-hero. Bartolomea was assigned
to watch her squirm.

At first, the priests believed. Back then, it wasn't, *Is this true?*
but, *Is this of God?* Fear and sadness meant Satan, but Benedetta
was joyful. She sat at the head of the table
and the other nuns did what she asked.

*6*

At dusk, the slightly older teens in charge sent us to bed
so they could sneak out and have sex in the cattails.
I occupied a small corner of the cabin, watched how easily
the other girls could touch each other's bare skin
as if it was nothing, like how my sister would cup
my small foot in her hand, paint flowers on my toenails.

I had no words for what I was, just thirst,
my throat so dry it wanted to exit itself.
*Through Him, with Him, in Him.* Be like them,
be with them, be in them. Bright bras

that left lines in their skin, bold as condensation trails
in blue sky. Forced myself to look away, aware
of my sin. Its hard, sharp shapes.

Benedetta starved, scrubbed her hands like she was searching
for proof of her own bones. Nuns fasted and washed
to be pure enough that Christ, the original Nice Guy, would want
to inhabit them. It's tempting to say they were anorexic,
like teenage girls in the early 2000s searching
for some kind of control, finding ways to lack, hacking open spaces

for boys to fill. But although the two realities hung over each other
like bunk beds, they weren't the same.
Benedetta wasn't interested in having a body,
her inferior realization of chromosomes, her reality

present there in the dark alongside those of us
who were not quite girls, but still desperate to be lived in.

Benedetta and Bartolomea fucked in the cloisters, the refectory,
the cellarium. In the kitchen, the orchard, docility
of the night stair. They fucked in the dormitory when Benedetta
was supposed to be receiving Christ's heart, her palms bloody
with manufactured stigmata. Bartolomea told the priests
she was catfished, how Christ sent his male angels to possess
Benedetta, make her look like a beautiful boy.

They imprisoned Benedetta in the convent for thirty-five years, until
    her quiet death.

Another sin: she had been eating in secret. Salami
and Cremonese mortadella were her favourites, their rush of salt.

9

The long dining hall was like an open throat that last morning,
its rough-hewn bones arching above me as I lined up for pancakes
made by someone's mom. At the far end of the room, Christ
watched me eat, his holes dripping syrup.

My father was an ex-Catholic atheist. He baptized me
with water from my mother's drinking glass minutes
after I was born, promised me to God, just in case.

Nobody told me I looked like my sister until after she was dead,
as if some shard of her was suddenly illuminated. Time and all its facets
existing alongside breakfast. Lighting up my skin like stained glass.

# SAILOR NEPTUNE TO SAILOR URANUS, 1998

Every day, we rocket unbuckled
in the backseat of my dad's

Pontiac Sunbird. Sharing headphones
on the way to soccer practice,

then sneaking into the movies,
where we inhale yards of red

licorice. Weighed down by wet
denim, we flip into the April river

when the ice is barely out, run home
through backyards, observed

by black cats. We shave Barbies
bald and zap each other

with carpet static, our electric
skin. Alone, we can transform: me,

into my own kind of magical girl, with eyes
that shoot lightning and a whip

made of Twizzlers. You, into a boy.
Someday, you'll be disinherited,

and I'll marry a man to prove
myself. For now, we sit behind

the Safeway eating ice cream in the shadow
of the green transformer. I scoop

from the middle, you lick
at the edges as they melt.

# I HAVE TO TELL HER THAT SHE WAS RIGHT

## Ash Wednesday

Her undeniable body scotched
between wall and misericord,
angel's face folded out
into a hard, wooden seat,
white rat in her pocket
while she sang hymn
after hymn and a dark cross
startled her forehead.

## Holy Thursday

Sixty heated metal swords
fell from the sky
like a Joan of Arc dream,
sluicing the earth at every downbeat
of her puzzled heart. Rain drummed
the bright glass and a boy wound
magenta gum into her hair,
his fingers slick as pews.

*Good Friday*

A group of Catholic schoolchildren
is called a witness. Gym floor ephemera
converged under their fingernails
while they watched the same stations
of the cross video every day
for forty days. She was there
and also separate. She was waiting
to explode from a tomb.

## Easter Vigil

Yellow-eyed against candle
glow, fingers templed. Flame
to her lips like dragon breath, Christ
flopped at the altar, plastic
piano keys shifting neatly. A girl
burned the tips of her hair,
strands lit up like gilded
shards of hymnal.

## Easter Sunday

Crocuses hid their corms
under frozen dirt, splotches
of purple spitting their orange stamens
at the sun. Other children whipped clods
of ice and brown rock at each other
below parking lot anti-abortion
billboards. She was not given
the chance to bleed.

## JANE TO HELEN, 2000

At a certain point in childhood, both of us,
with our uneven haircuts, realize that to earn

love we must learn to be Real Girls. So we study
*Cosmo* and *Teen Vogue*, wiggle mascara wands

to prevent clumping, and trade colourful
Northern Getaway sweatpants for low-rise

jeans and overpriced American Eagle. Still,
we can't stuff down our aching

strangeness. The changeling myth is thought,
by some, to have been inspired by autistic

children. Such happy babies we were,
said our mothers, until one day a faraway look

invaded our eyes, and we were no longer easy.
Our struggle contained, little sparks

from our bright filaments. We didn't know
that the fairies brought us to our real selves

and that "girl" was a mask
we would learn to wear well.

## LILITH TO EVE, 2001

Remember how we went online every night
in your grandma's attic, showed our pubescent

tits to the early-2000s internet? Do you ever
wonder if we still feature among the terabytes

of CSAM floating around this fuckhole world?
I once found you up there, shirt off,

monitor's glow making you a *Law & Order*
corpse. You had the face of the man

watching you covered with a purple Post-it. *It's easier
if you can't see them*, you told me. Later,

we snuck out, walked to the house of a friend
whose mom was never home. His older brother

bought beer, and the boys got drunk
and watched us kiss. We didn't talk

on the way home through the snow-quiet
suburbs. You're still in town with your couple

of kids; we almost hung out once, but you bailed
at the last minute, never spoke to me again.

You must think it would do us no good
to return to our dark mythology.

# AGUSTINA TO THE VIRGIN MARY, 2004

*For this thing I besought the Lord thrice, that it might depart from me.*
—2 Cor. 12:8

A single thorn would leave a wound
like the Romans left in Christ: throbbing,

red-wet, vulvic. Uncongenial splinter,
octaves-long and so easily pluckable.

Ours are small as sesame seeds, frequent
as sounds. Infinite drains to soak

our flesh in bright water, like a miracle
or the weeping of stone.

# MARIANNE

Her brother's wife died in the winter of 1960,
seven children left behind and the northern ground
too frozen to dig a grave. She might have driven
her El Camino south to California, where her army
buddies kept ferocious acres; instead, she arrived
with her leather Samsonite on the doorstep of 1014
Second Street, its two small bedrooms.

The third eldest—my mother, not quite ten—
was curled into a paperback. Marianne told her
that if she had nothing to do, the baseboards
could always be dusted. Girls pulled frozen
laundry from the line, numbed their grieving
hands; stiff jeans and jackets stood melting
in the kitchen, like people trying to exist.

Marianne bought a cabin on Northwest Bay,
baby toads on the beach at sunset, children's
feet coated in cold sand. Boys chopped wood
and whistled duck sounds through grass,
her *Quiet down* lost on the wind. At midnight,
she'd wake to feed the woodstove, adjust
a stray blanket. Her distant warmth.

She might have dreamed: crosswords in bed,
tomatoes on toast. A beloved illuminated
by grocery store carnations. My own closeted
desires; I offer them now, posthumous
gifts. Tell myself a story about her, alone
with the juniper. Eyes closed, sun clattering red
shapes of pleasure inside her pink lids.

## FIELD PARTY

Northern springtime, high school boys in ritual darkness make a pile
of last year's Christmas trees, swallow their dads' back pills with
   Budweiser.

Encircled with light and girls and cattle breathing as one creature
in the black beyond, the boys buck back and forth through ribbons
   of flame,

making mud of brown grass. Girls must help the injured, as cattle
must make milk and meat. Up in the house's carpeted bathroom, a boy

rests his chin in my hand, his eyes bloodshot as berries. Peeling
wallpaper lambs hang over us like sacrifice. I anoint him with Visine,

put a cold hand to his burning cheek. Thirteen years later in another
northern May, I will see his name on a list of local men arrested

for sex trafficking. Will I regret the tenderness? My daughter
is big enough to build a fire. Our bodies ominous as springsoft ice.

## ANNE TO DIANA, 2008

At our asymmetrical confluence,
all soft arches, searching the heavy

soak below sand for a shambles
community of those nihilists called

snuffbox, round pigtoe, northern
riffleshell. Pearl of meat between

the sharp spread of pocketbook,
tannic smell of tasteless flesh

pushing back
against a teething.

# HOW QUEER AND QUIET IT IS

*Disappearing into Edenic homosociality held great appeal for Burnett;*
*later in life she wrote of "holding as my most fixed creed that not to [be]*
*married was Paradise" and her last significant relationship was with a*
*woman, Elizabeth Jordan. They called each other "Querida" ("Dearest")*
*or—resonantly—Q.*
—Kate Thomas

1

We are queer children,
and no one will admit it.
We go to different churches,
and though we live in the same small
town, we will not meet for many years.

Our mothers keep fenced gardens.
Like us, they don't belong to themselves
or the world.

We learn to contain: this feeling,
that feeling. Mostly anger.
What matters is that we are good,
quiet girls, fulfill the promise
of our mothers, who built us
on the lobed altars of their placentae.

They read to us about bedridden
children, orphans, evenings
when we twist our young bodies
in queer ways nobody sees.

2

The word "queer"
appears sixty-one times
in *The Secret Garden*, so we know
our mothers' voices made
the sound, though we don't
remember hearing it.

We develop a queer way of seeing:
through robins. They fly back
and forth between our houses,
tasting the water from each mother's
stone birdbath, dust of us
on their wings.

3

There are places where it feels,
at least, like we are not being
witnessed: islands of swelling
grasses, granite moors, fermented
tang of fallen berries. Around every corner,
an imaginary hut kept warm by woodstove
where we might live unobserved.

We don't remember how we once met
there, blackflies
nipping our bare ankles
and the incongruent smell
of coconut sunscreen.

It's true because it's written here.
We were two queer children,
seeing each other.

4

Frances wrote another story
called "In the Closed Room," about two
little girls who find each other
outside a garden.

They're called through the gate
by an aunt, who's queer
and therefore dead.
She knows the girls
by seeing them, invites them
into paradise. Queerness,
then, is inherited doom.

5

We each knew one gay man,
no lesbians. To be clear,
no one ever told us the man was gay.
To be clear, we saw women
who our fathers, brothers,
cousins, friends
might call *dyke*.

There was no way forward;
thoughts could never fully form.
No way to trade in the love mined
from years of being good
girls. Feelings came
in flashes, like smears
of open field out the window.

6

The illustrator of "In the Closed Room"
was a queer woman who fled
into nature with other queer
women. In a photo,
three hold paper roses
while a fourth poses above them
with a watering can.

Our own queer aunts
hide around us in plain sight,
with their roommates
and gold Gemini pendants,
two women hiding their embrace
behind the idea of twins.

We weren't meant
to be lovers, but still,
if we had found each other
sooner. Like in a garden.

7

At dance class and gymnastics, girls
sit in circles, tickling
each other's backs.
We keep our predatory
hands cornered.

On class trips, we haunt hotel
hallways, watch other girls
in their glasses and pajamas,
artifice of school stripped away.
The word "girlfriend" is unsexed
and can be said freely,
though it rings hollow
in our chests.

This kind of echo is a pain
we will return to.

*8*

Closeted queer girls in northwestern Ontario
date boys who embody
something of queerness,
who are gentle,
know animal calls,
loon sounds whistled
through cupped palms.

More than anything,
they are freer than us,
so in pinning them down
we grasp at something
of ourselves.

*9*

We are not of our families. We stare
at walls, like animals
seeming fixated on nothing,
but clearly seeing ghosts.

We bend our pale fingers back
like dolls put together wrong
while our mothers watch
the moon, misunderstanding
its phases.

They can't give us
what we need of them.
Their memories are glossed
in lamplight.

The girls from "In the Closed Room"
leave their mothers easily,
choose the delight
of death's garden
over living unseen.

*10*

We hate and envy children
who can't hide their queerness;
sheathed in dresses, we reject
the liminal space at the edge
of our vision. We don't know
that we know that this scab
is queer. That breeze.
This sonnet, that bridge.
That painter, this smell
of orange oil, this flower,
its petals like flesh.

*11*

We are mature
until we aren't,
told all our lives
that we have "old souls."
We are the grown-up,
trustworthy girls
we were asked to be
until we overflow,
give ourselves to boys,
then men,
who become un-gentle
when they can't absorb
the spill.

We begin our search
for the release
of some other landscape.

*12*

We marry young, have babies
with men we love
like through winter-frosted
glass. Cold peace
of being good girls
forever, giving our mothers
what they trained us to give.

Most characters in *The Secret Garden*
are at one time or another
described as queer
or as having queer voices,
queer mannerisms.

We read it to our children,
censor each *queer* into *strange,*
little acts of violence.

13

Van-lifers and Instagram tiny-housers
multiply. Now separated
by only two short blocks, we build
similar search histories:
*Lesbian commune.*
*Active queer intentional community.*
We are fastened to our homes
by husbands, children,
asking ourselves if it's possible
to know before the knowing
has been made safe.

What is a garden if not
a proliferation of tongues,
living volta of petal
layers parting to a fuzzy
pollen heart.

What is queerness
if not crabbed tenderness,
shrewd understanding.

What is queer knowing,
if not an unnameable vortex
of some things human
and some, beyond.

Finally, we arrive
at our splitting: I leave
my husband,
and you stay.

We each contain
a queer child,
rambling freely.
They look out
at each other
through our open eyes.

*16*

In our shared
community plot,
our children sing,
stain their lips with raspberries.
Cup shining grubs
from rich earth.

We marvel at the mirror
of our lives, how our bodies
belong to our children,
our minds
to our mothers.

*17*

Woods swell green and lush
around us, our laughter catching
into yawns, simultaneous
and gaping, a queer
intake of breath.

We know we don't own
our children. We've made
gates of ourselves,
key unburied
and hung by a hook.

## LORENA TO ELEANOR, 2009

I count the rungs of your ribcage
as you climb into the hayloft. Field

sparrows gather in the big bluestem,
listen as you finger my hair

into a French braid. Below us, an array
of leather harnesses, prairie hushed

and constant, listening. I'll never out
you; I've self-redacted. Cityside, I crunch

down on your name's triple syllables, offer
you in coffee shops, prelude to bitterness.

Think of the soft spot just northeast
of the corner of your mouth against my lips.

# WALL OF SOUND

*for Brian Wilson*

I hear them too, Brian. Demons
in the headphones. What came first, the brain
or the drugs? Brain or the damage?

Bad vibrations, like the kind our mothers
warned us about. Don't get near the man
who can't make friends with dogs. Once,
my big brother had a breakdown
in an art gallery looking
at a violence of rainbows.

You write songs like therapy, Brian.
Parts layered on parts, a pocket
symphony. I think of my own sections.

Art always bumps against insecure
brain bonds, and it's hard not to connect,
like when you first heard Phil Spector
and recognized your inner clicks
in a song sung by his second wife
and without that, no this.

Called non-verbal behind
your wall of sound as if theremin,
as if cello weren't speaking.
My undiagnosed child-self
responds to the buzz,
tender in road trip backseats.

Gentle bitter of Lorazepam,
how we wish these brains
made their own calm.

Without this, no that. Ronnie Spector
escaped barefoot, forfeited fortune
and custody to her husband,
who was going to kill her,
who did bad things to their children.

The music collects its fragments.
Endless as *la la la*.

# RABBIT'S MOON

Anger pours through celluloid, theatre
soaked in blue. Beside me, my brother
watches the clown die
reaching for the Rabbit God.

At the bar, he tells me
he will never speak to our father
again, traces his temper to the sudden
rages of our childhood.
He can no longer make shapes
from the dust of care.

Neon blues our pale
beer. I don't want to talk
about plot, so I answer
by explaining how Kenneth,
the director, changed his name
to Anger after being arrested
for homosexual entrapment.
His rabbit was the god
of queer sex.

We have always spoken to each other
in protective mechanisms,
like a silent movie dubbed
with contrary pop. He rejects
the blueness of our father's
eyes, how they occupy his own.

My brother has given up
reaching. I have watched him
wanting to hit his own small
child. Maybe, sometimes,
he does. Fear on his face,
like the moon is gone.

## EMILY TO SUSAN, 2011

Twilight minutes tick by, little flicks
of the clock, gloam kneading its ink

into City Hall and Cambie lit up
beyond. Hummingbirds at your gate dip

their sonic tongues into night-blooming
jasmine's waiting chambers, air thick

as nectar. Your shadow floods the window;
my anxious fingers thrum.

# I'M NOT A HUMAN I'M THREE POEMS IN
## A TRENCH COAT

I was at the mall, trying to write a poem
about a radish. It wasn't going well.
For some reason, I had a boyfriend.

He wasn't there, so I rode up
the long escalator, past the crystal dragon
store's many wizards,
knocked on the movie theatre's neon
lips. The teenage attendants
were easily fooled by my stacks
of pages. Told them not to worry;
I didn't like myself enough to spell
my name with popcorn
on an empty seat.

After the credits, my throat itched
with trapped noise. I walked
to the train station, warm rain wetting
rails and the far-off sound
of metal. A man carried a jackfruit
the size of my head under his arm.
*Maybe that's a poem*, I thought.

*I toss the stone of my story into a vast crevice; measure the emptiness by its*
*small sound.*
—Carmen Maria Machado

Halloween lanterns ignite the damp
lawn, your mother's distant clock

pounding midnight. You kept me
awake until I kissed the kitchen

knife with my own thigh's flesh,
dragged me here in a fit of thirst.

When we first met, you said
you'd seen my face in a dream,

your pony-bright eyes flickering.
I wanted to whisper your deity's name

to you in the dark, feel its long
vowels exhale against the insides

of my cheeks. Despite your violence,
I was not trained to believe a woman

could do this to me. Plastic ghosts
are my only witnesses; they watch

you press your face to the wound I made
for you, baring my deadname like a tooth.

# ORLANDO TO SASHA, 2013

We don't know how dragonflies die. Find their bodies
on rock cuts in the sun, crusts of their former

selves, entire beings turned skeleton. For a funeral,
crush them into iridescent dust and blow their glitter

across the lake. Haskaps ripen hourly in the blasted
heat, screams of grasshoppers rise to an eerie

crescendo. I metamorphose for you
in the long grass while globe thistle looks on,

its enviable pointed orbs. What do you need,
my darling? Protection of the jack pine? Endless

hip and tongue of the garter snake? He leaves
his rough scent in your hair. The time of violets

has passed, their sweet openings. We'll know
a gasping winter before we see them again.

## TAM TO SALLY, 2014

You tell me about space junk, orbital flotsam. Cameras,
pliers, wrenches. An astronaut's glove. Spatula coated

with a thin layer of cosmic egg. Seven million kilograms
of trash, large as spent rockets and small as flakes of paint,

scattered like birdseed across Earth's equatorial plane.
Living satellites revolve gently through a graveyard

of their deceased ancestors, knowing one day
they will have to fall. Down here, we lie next to each other

in bed, and this is the entirety of the universe.
I'm looking at a moon phases app on my phone,

trying not to imagine the impossibly heavy sky
of metal and fuselage floating between us and heaven.

## CANDY HOUSE

We used to party here. Small town
high school Halloween, sequined devil
horns, floor overgrown with used
condoms and candy wrappers. Wet
marshmallow smell, walls lit
by crescent moon's waning blade,
spray paint bloody, leaking licorice
wires. Jaw greening in the shape
of my boyfriend's fist, my flesh
discarded, pale and hard
as peppermint, sugar dusted,
sweating syrup. Beams spread
raw, spilling fairy floss viscera
that drifts up into chokecherry
branches, its BE MINE blooms,
leaves cyanotic. I remember
blue-raspberry tongues. Time
when I could eat whatever I wanted.

I'm sleeping. We're sixteen, listening to "Several Small Animals"
and admiring the several small animals he brings:
wounded whisky jacks, luna moths, plastic bags
full of bright fish. Rubs white pills
between his fingertips, embeds them
in my memory, seeds of a future dream.

I'm sleeping. He lets himself in through the library door.
He's been gone for nine years and I wasn't
expecting him; bloodless fingers, cool skin
shining like my nightmares of his recurring
death. I do as I've been taught and kiss him
until he seems real.

I'm sleeping, mouth open. Festival of snowflakes lets loose
onto my tongue in his parents' hot tub, "Silverbells" aching
through the waterproof speakers. I propose to him,
flakes dying like fairies in the heat. He takes me
up to his childhood bedroom, ties me to the bed
with a bass amp cord.

I'm sleeping. Deliver him daily to the OATC, watch him
through a rip in the reflective window covering. O
a brilliant void above me, full moon
obscured by snow-fattened clouds. After,
he asks me if I want to steal a lawn ornament,
as if a decade hasn't passed.

I'm sleeping. He gives me a brief son. Shards of brown snow
heap around us at the hospital, layered like time.
We are children and married and ended
in the space of a second, constant shape
of syringe in his pocket. I can't wake up,
even after pricking my finger on the tip.

# THE WITCH IN THE STONE BOAT

*after an Icelandic fairy tale*

High noon shreds the fibres of my lips. Empty cooler
floating insect limbs: wing of fly, leg of spider. Stringer
of walleye apathetic off the port side, colour fading
from their bodies as they bump against the hull, nylon
slimed through their tender jaws. My husband casts
from his camo seat, testicle leaking from his camo
shorts. Sweat lagooning philtrum. Her shape

overtakes the horizon, swift as terror, skimming
still water on solid granite. Dynamite blasted like rock
cuts, all arm muscle, her shoulders roiling like a nest
of snakes. Her skin is furred like fresh antler and makes
its own daytime. Seen only by me, she comes aboard,
drops a fish's eye behind my teeth. I explore its jelly
edges with my tongue. At home,

a woman with my face rises through the floor. I want her
to leave, but she hovers in the hallway like a light
fixture. I divorce pickerel from their skins, squinting
in the glow of her skirts. My husband tells me I should hang
more of her. I yawn, and his screaming is a mirror;
he can see the witch inside, my throat widening
like a cervix to release her.

## CALLISTO TO ARTEMIS, 2015

Webbed in wires, belly waxing
and a winter storm wiping out

the moon. Open on the table,
my uterus orbiting the room

like a lost comet, they told me
the baby was sideways.

We would have died, had you
not appeared as a celestial bear

to wrench us from the dark
river, give us a home on Earth.

Still dark in Montréal as we make
our way to the clinic by cab, past phallic

cathedral spires waiting for dawn
to purple them into being. Building

is 1990s brutalism, a mouthful
of concrete teeth and teal linoleum.

Nurses call you "he" and "sir,"
another penance for your desire

to be breastless. After they wheel
you away, I pick up your jeans

to fold them, and they surrender
constellations of coins and small

screws onto the gritty floor;
your undeniable astrology.

I fall asleep in a chair, dream
that I can hear your flesh

thumping into the floor above me.
Later, at the hotel, you are supposed

to be resting, though we can't help
but touch each other

in the biohazard glow of your new,
supernatural form.

OVERBOARD

Harlequin Great Dane topples
from our patient's mobile home
at the sound of ambulance tires
down gravel drive. Wipers
snapping, Beauty Bay's water
frantic in the shadow
of the neighbour's airplane
hangar. Outrageous dog
vermiculating across the lawn,
impossible cow, its sepulchral
chest. Black and white
like Goldie Hawn's swimsuit
in *Overboard* that showed all
of her vulva but the slit. Patient
at the door, colossally pregnant,
voice snatched by her neighbour's
amphibious aircraft taking off
across the water on keen
pontoons. Are we all leaning
into the vibration? Walls
and bloody shelves of our bodies
pulsing, shock of sympathy
contractions, dog now hurling its body
at the lake. Blood chucking it
down the rift in our patient's
bathrobe, silent light show
behind us. Everything
about to split.

## ELSIE TO ELIZABETH, 2016

Death to William Morris! Death
to my father's silk drapes shut

over windows of Victoriana, his mahogany
mantles and button-backed chairs, rooms

claimed by men who offer wigs and pink
tights as their cast-offs. Give me

head on a leopard-print chaise longue
while bursts of god-faces watch, ticking

of ridiculous clocks. Chinoiserie
and chintz, floor-to-ceiling indoor trellises,

lascivious aquamarine. Wicker, green
and white, *trompe l'oeil* as we are.

Death to *oh my god, they were roommates.*
Home in our rococo womb.

# WINTER SONG

*after Joy Harjo*

I walk with a friend
in the bright cold.
Fingers of light knit the loose fibres
of her wool sweater.
We are like the creek,
how we resist hardening.
Things as small as noticing,
as supposedly natural as pleasure,
feel out of reach.
Snow balances divinely in the air.
If we look behind us, if we hear
what might be a footstep,
we will run. I put myself
between my friend
and the empty woods at her back.
The day allows our passage,
eagles circling the low sun
and the two of us,
alive together.

## APHRODITE TO SAPPHO, 2017

Pale green of sea-dusk on Lake Huron, crush
of zebra mussels, fragile coffins. Stars

like branches of malachite cast their acicular
beams, stringers of light dripping down

the backs of our necks. All day I collected
samples of humanity's myopia along receding

coastline, and I've become voracious. Let me
lay you down on this bed of invasive species,

exalt in your many ridged ceilings. Send a prayer
to Oceanus that we might somehow braid

our DNA, give birth to a clutch of coral orbs,
a restoration of trout, skins freckled and sleek.

# I AM ONCE AGAIN ASKING IF I AM TOO MUCH

After the negative pregnancy test, I drop
my daughter off at Lego Club where she eats cupcakes
with three other girls, lips stained neon
pink with airbrush icing, laughter interrupting
the dull office where they meet.

I take a walk, listen to "If I Were a Carpenter." My most-walked
block, but somehow, there are blue shutters
I have never seen, hearts cut roughly
from their centres, sheltering an attic window.

Before I told you I was late, we looked at houses
on your phone, a weekly ritual. Two-storey Victorian
in your hometown, butter-yellow. I will think about that house
for weeks; no houses like it here. I have begun to realize
some futures are lost to me.

At the end of my walk, I text you. A couple
is chasing a white chicken around the parking lot;
the man rolls his eyes at the woman, lovingly.

Later, my daughter is sleeping in her room the colour
of an unopened violet, her stars-and-moons blanket replaced
by my ex's old comforter. I tuck in her bare leg and wait
for the rise of her chest, thinking how I loved her
when I was twenty-three and alone,
and she was barely a thought.

You are waiting to show me more houses. Soon,
you will buy a place of your own, move out of your grey apartment
with its always-drawn blinds. I know you wouldn't feel sad
about something that never existed,
that neither of us wants. But you would hold open
a room for my sadness. Linger
in the doorway, listening for breath.

## YARDWORK

It was the child screaming at the screen door,
       how her bellow was stolen by the roaring
train, two men fist-fighting on the other side
       of the fence. It was also the rainless summer
storm railing dust into its swollen nostrils,
       high deforestation gale, forest fire skies
and the doom-orange sun like Sauron's eye.
       It was *faggot* barked like a mower blade
breaking against bedrock while the train, still heaving
       past behind the Beer Store, yelped sparks
into the dry grass. It was the wind, whipping
       the house with endless flyers from the No Frills
parking lot. Mostly, it was the brown baby gull
       I found dead under the stinging nettle. How
I didn't call the cops but they came anyway, loaded
       bodies into their white van, child watching.

## AMY TO ADA, 2018

You come home from work at dawn,
smelling of hospital. I'm waiting

in the quiet of the raised beds you built,
admiring how morning sun transforms

the tomatoes. What has followed you
here today? Your insides frantic

with ambulance lights. The snap
pea wears its calyx like a wee hat;

you peel it back, expose the aching
fruit inside while already, another

set of sirens is keening by.
Our daughter's fairy face appears

above us, calling down from her window
like Rapunzel. I follow you inside.

# PHONE APPOINTMENT

He won't hear
of my bleeding; it's what

I'm bred for. To collapse
in the grocery store

is to be alive in this body,
trail of blood

and milk. Miscarried
five years ago, now

I hemorrhage every
month, new curse. He

suggests Naproxen
again, as a clot the size

of my fist slips
from me. Won't waste

taxpayer money on
another test, won't accept

more of my blood,
through vagina or

vial. My hands are full
of viscera so I put him

on speaker with the tip
of my nose. *Any pain?*

he asks, but what's
the point in saying yes.

# GIRLDEFINED

*These Texas gals are passionate about God's beautiful design for womanhood …*
— Girldefined.com

Blonde godheads, god girls, proselytizing
YouTube doll babies. Their blog favicon

a white-panty period stain. Sweet girls,
what do they desire? Girldefined, ecstatic

girl-tongue. Girl is Jesus's daughter and his
wife. White Jesus with pecs and a six

pack, blank Ken-doll genitals. *God
Made You Beautiful, Despite*

*How Ugly You Feel.* How nice that was
of God. He defined girl; God said girl

is a hole to spit in. God girls want to get
thumped by God's beam-of-light

cock. Girldefined sisters, sister-wives
of Christ, trying to get him hard,

but the world's aborted fetuses are God's
anti-Viagra. God girls see me

in their analytics, typing *lesbian*
into the search bar. Not defined here

as girl. Girldefined girls define God
so literally. He's a dude in a basement

with a sign that says *Man Cave.*
Hard at work creating the pussy.

UGLY PUSSY

Poetry bros at the poetry festival are visibly
uncomfortable while I read my poem,
"Ugly Pussy." I guess it's not fair for me
to expect them to get it. For all that I've studied
poetry, I haven't *studied* poetry, and I find myself
needing them to mansplain their twisting
metaphors as they float above my head, passing
like clouds over my lowly register. Poetry bros
know they're supposed to respect me, so they come up
with a question: *Was that sonnet form?*
No, it was a poem about how a boy called me
ugly pussy behind the French portable in grade seven,
and poetry is how my trash mind processes
such incidents. Of course, there is a little thing called craft.
Mine shoots lasers.
*Pew pew!*

CHECK ALL THAT APPLY

I was tasked with teaching Catholic school preteens about gender.
Inevitably, they asked, *So you can just identify as ANYTHING?*
*I'm a dog, everyone! I'm an airplane!*

Why not? I think I might be a translucent lobster that only leaves
its mud-home on the full moon. Or an albino cow moose crowned
in marigolds. Renaissance baby, 1970s carpet sample. Sometimes,
I identify as made-up band names, like Bitter Herb and the Rejected
Gourds. Sometimes I feel like the back end of a hatchet.

What about a box on all intake forms that reads:
*Prefers not to be perceived?* Or the three genders: man, woman,
demon. What if I identify as a gender reveal, the kind with explosions
that start forest fires? Or a photo of my clearly queer self at their age.

I think, after all, I'm the circles.
Little blank voids, full of terror.

## YOUR WIFE IS A CRYPTID

They ugly over a pot
of stinging nettle, their medicine
a threat to domination,
picking crusts of period
blood from their pubic hair
to help them think. They are taller
than two men, trauma stacked
on trauma wrapped
in faux leather that when removed
reveals a swarm of bees. Your wife
looks pissed in grainy pictures
on a shitty Samsung phone,
and when you show them
to other people, all they see
is woods. They squeeze ingrown hairs
from your elbows, bumps
in the night, they have no insurance. Make
you swallow foul tinctures
when your uterus cramps. They save
the contents of their blackheads
for you. Your wife
is burnt-out forests. Their guts
are filled with sour ghosts.

## OH MY GOSH ... HAVE WE GOT SQUASH

*for T.W. King*

*Gardens and farms sometimes yield well. Often times,*
*they don't.* The same could be said about poets, T.W.
Your face at the Zoom reading, bright as a pumpkin.
*We have fun,* you say of yourself and your wife, lanky
pines of your Wisconsin homestead watching
you self-publish thirteen books in the last two years alone.
T.W., I'm obsessed with you, sincerely. Honoured
your disabled sister with a career engineering
adaptive technologies, worked with Stephen Hawking
and still write textbooks when you're not writing
poems. Self-aware about your rhyming squash
chapbook, you say, *I just hope to make you smile.*
You saw that orange and yellow bounty, T.W.,
and nothing could stop you from writing a book
about it. You have fun. I'm making your book
my bible; tell me everything about Mr. Beauregard
and his wife Beatrix, your angora rabbits who love
to watch hockey. How you write poems
about sheep farming on your way to the post office.
You perform raps about tick safety for second graders,
and one for tortured writers reminding us *our dirt nap's comin'*
so we better get on with it. *Gotta wet the mechanism,*
you say as you take a sip of water, end gently
with your sister who loved to swing for hours
among the pines. You make me want to write about joy.

# MRS. MIDWEST

*A feminine homemaker blogging on women's issues.*
—MrsMidwest.com

Mrs. redpill tradwife, Mrs. blue life. White
WIFEY mug, Titus 2 woman, Instagram bio

scripture and a Following list flush
with ~*aesthetic*~ neo-Nazis. Mrs. green

lawn, Mrs. naturally blonde. Mrs. listicle
writer: *5 Ways to Be More Feminine Today!*

*4 Ways I Help My Husband Lead Me.*
Mrs. NiceGuys™ in the analytics,

Mrs. god-honouring OnlyFans, posting
for incels on 4chan: *My husband listens*

*when I want to chat about the frustrations*
*of finding attractive clothing for a larger bust.*

Mrs. little old me with a marketing
degree. FAQ: *How tall are you?*

A: *5'8"! I wish I was shorter…*
same MANLY height as I am, Mrs.

if we kissed? Mrs. Reddit confessor,
crushed on an all-girls-camp counsellor

in high school, Mrs. I would never
act on it. Mrs. love the sinner, hate

the sin. Mrs. Church emoji, Mrs. Leaf
Fluttering in the Wind.

## LOUISA MAY TO ANNE, 2022

Days before our camping trip, you googled
*Thoreau's queerest poems.* Funny, how far

you were from mushrooms. Texted me,
playfully, *Bring that tongue on Sunday,*

and Siri popped up a suggested reminder.
On the flat top of a red cliff, we look out

at the Sleeping Giant, eat our powdered
food from plastic discs. We won't afford

our own place in the woods of this stolen
land; everything's owned by Americans,

Manitobans, hockey players who visit
once a year. I redraft my novel, our toes

in Lake Superior, and you tell me
how Thoreau once accidentally set fire

to eight hundred valuable acres
while on a date with another man. *That's gay*

*panic.* At night, you rub the stiffness
from my forearms, read passages

from *Walden.* Wrap your mouth
around the lit end of a flashlight

like children do. Here, we are
children. We are lit from within.

## NOTES

Sunny Cove is a camp on Rainy Lake in northwestern Ontario.

OATC stands for Ontario Addiction Treatment Centre.

CSAM stands for Child Sexual Abuse Material.

In 2 Corinthians 12:8, Paul reveals that he has begged God three times to remove his unnamed deficiency.

"Oh my god, they were roommates" refers to an infamous Vine by the user @mattsukkar.

Snuffbox, round pigtoe, northern riffleshell and pocketbook are all mollusks found in northern Ontario.

"Soft spot just northeast of the corner of your mouth against my lips" is a line borrowed from a letter from Lorena Hickok to Eleanor Roosevelt in 1933.

"In the Closed Room" by Frances Hodgson Burnett was illustrated by Jessie Willcox Smith. She was one third of the "Red Rose Girls," along with Elizabeth Shippen Green and Violet Oakley. They named themselves after the Red Rose Inn in Villanova, Pennsylvania, where they lived and worked together for many years.

"There was a mixture of crabbed tenderness and shrewd understanding in his manner" is a line from *The Secret Garden* describing the character Ben Weatherstaff.

"The three genders: man, woman, demon" refers to the broader "Ah, yes, the three genders" meme.

*Oh My Gosh … Have We Got Squash!: Rhymes, Raps, and Stories from Gardens and Farms* is a 2021 book by Debra Raye King and Thomas Wayne King.

## BIBLIOGRAPHY

I read widely while writing this book. Here, I'm including works that furthered my understanding of existent texts and provided invaluable historical context for the subjects that inspired these poems.

Brown, Judith C. *Immodest Acts: The Life of a Lesbian Nun in Renaissance Italy*. Oxford University Press, 1986.

Faderman, Lillian. *Surpassing the Love of Men: Romantic Friendship and Love Between Women from the Renaissance to the Present*. HarperCollins, 1981.

Le Fanu, Joseph Sheridan. *Carmilla*. Edited by Carmen Maria Machado. Lanternfish Press, 2019.

Patrick-West, Grace. "The Realm of Faeries: Queerness and Neurodivergence in Jane Eyre." *Central College*, 2021.

Rupp, Leila J. *Sapphistries: A Global History of Love Between Women*. New York University Press, 2009.

Thomas, Kate. "Eternal Gardens and the Queer Uncanny in Frances Hodgson Burnett's 'In the Closed Room' (1902)." *Pacific Coast Philology* 50, no. 2, Special Issue: Familiar Spirits (December 2015): 173–183.

## ACKNOWLEDGEMENTS

Poems from this book first appeared in *Qwerty*, *EVENT Magazine*, *Contemporary Verse 2*, *SICK Magazine*, *Plenitude Magazine* and *Poetry is Dead Magazine*. Thank you to the editors of each.

This project was supported by the Canada Council for the Arts and the Ontario Arts Council.

Thank you to everyone at Nightwood Editions for their hard work and for believing in this book. Thanks especially to Janine Young for encouragement, invaluable editorial insights and for giving me a sense of being understood.

"I Have to Tell Her That She Was Right" borrows its title from the last line of "Poem for a Lonely Girl" by Ruth Daniell, and was inspired both by Ruth's poetry and her visual art. Ruth, thank you for making art with me, dreaming with me and being my friend. My work wouldn't be what it is without your guidance and inspiration.

Thank you to Ellie Sawatzky, sister of my heart, forever first reader and beloved lifelong confidante. I am endlessly grateful to poetry for bringing us together.

Thank you to Jennifer Krag for loving me so well that the love turns to poetry.

Thank you to my parents, Cis and Bob Barron, for nurturing my tendency to dream. Thank you also to my entire extended family—aunties, uncles, cousins—I love you.

Love and gratitude to Adam Bertolo, August Bourré, Adrick Brock, Reece Cochrane, Nadine Cousineau, Rhonda Douglas, Evan J, Donna Kane, Cara Kauhane, Erin Kirsh, Josh Loeser, Paul Moorehead, George Murray, Whitney O'Donnell, df parizeau, Heather Ramsay, Paul Robichaud, Erin Stainsby-Anderson, John Elizabeth Stintzi, Rhea Tregebov and Jonathan Woodcock.

Anouk: You will read this one day and know that of all the loves in my life, you are the greatest.

## ABOUT THE AUTHOR

Joelle Barron is an award-winning poet and writer living and relying on the Traditional Territory of the Anishinaabeg of Treaty 3 and the Métis people (Fort Frances, ON). Their first poetry collection, *Ritual Lights* (icehouse poetry, 2018), was nominated for the Gerald Lampert Memorial Award. In 2019, they were a finalist for the Dayne Ogilvie Prize for Emerging LGBTQ2S+ Writers. Joelle's poetry has appeared in *ARC Poetry Magazine, CV2, EVENT Magazine, The New Quarterly* and many other Canadian literary publications. They live with their daughter.